I Will Not
Be Denied

by

Evangelist Shirley Pruitt

ISBN-979-8-9865839-5-2

House of Stone Publishing
Macon - Georgia

I Will Not
Be Denied

Table of Content

Dedication

This book is dedicated to my Lord and Savior Jesus Christ, whom I thank every day for
giving me another chance and the strength to get up and start again. Thank you Jesus!

In loving memory of my mother, Mother Odessa Curtiss Pruitt. Thank you for leaving me a legacy of how a godly woman should live; a life by precepts and examples. And for also being a mighty powerful praying woman of God; thank you mama. Hoping and praying to see you again, where heaven will be our final destination and eternal home. Love you mama.

To my one and only daughter, Mrs. Aleika J. Barnes Luckett, this book is dedicated to you as well. Thank you for your prayers, support and being my best friend and confidant. For encouraging me to continue to write this book when I would get discouraged and wanted to give up. Thank you for being there for me when I was at my lowest end. You were never afraid to show me tough love when I needed it. Thank you for your love, strength, courage, boldness and respect; while still allowing me to be mama. Most of all, I thank you for allowing the Lord to make you that Proverbs 31 woman that the Bible speaks of. From day to day, God has allowed it to be fulfilled before my eyes. Thank you for being my Pastor. I love you Niki.

೫ Introduction

This book was birthed during a time of many transitions in my life, both physical and spiritual. I was at a cross road and many decisions were to be made. In June 1998, it seemed that life as I knew it was collapsing all around me. Many problems were pulling me down like a pool of quicksand and there was no way out. The things that I had put so much time and effort in were diminishing very rapidly. My mind was running in all directions, wondering who would pull me out of this dilemma. At that moment my mind reflected on Scriptures that my mother had taught me during some of the hardships she had endured in life.

In the Book of Romans the seventh chapter and the twenty-fourth verse, reads, (KJV) "O wretched man that I am! who shall deliver me from the body of this death?" Confused, hurt, disappointed and discouraged, I asked myself what's next. While waiting for the answer other Scriptures began to flood my mind. Psalm 18:6 (KJV) declares, "In my distress I called upon the LORD, and cried unto my God: he heard my voice out of his temple, and my cry came before him, even into his ears." Psalm 34:4 declares, "I sought the LORD, and he heard me, and delivered me from all my fears." As I meditated on those Scriptures, I began to feel better, my spirit was lifted and my mind clearer. At that moment my life began to change as rapidly as it was collapsing. I thank the Lord for sending His Word, healing and delivering me from my destruction (Psalm 107:20).

I must say that if we hide the Word in our hearts, in the time of trouble the Lord will bring it back to our remembrance. Things began to turn around for me and a new life of purpose sprang forth from dilemma to deliverance. This is why I can say, "I will not be denied." I hope and pray that this book will be an inspiration to all of you who read it, as well as it was for me to write it. My prayer is that you be willing to allow the Holy Spirit to lead, guide and direct you; fulfilling the purpose that The Lord has for your life.

Your sister in Christ, Evangelist Shirley A. Pruitt

⟆ Humble Beginnings

Sitting at the kitchen table, propped up on one elbow; I sat there wondering if life had played a big joke on me. I was thinking all was lost. The one exception and bright spot of my life were my five wonderful children. They were a blessing from the Lord. Over the years I had become tired, drained and empty. I truly believed that I didn't have anything else to give. I had given of myself, over and over again. I wondered if this was it. I was feeling like life had thrown me a curb ball and I had struck out. I really wondered if it was over for me. My thinking began to shift a bit as I considered what someone had said to me; "It's not over until God says it's over".

Despite remembering these words, I was still entertaining my negative thoughts about the curb ball. Could I have hit a homerun, if I was more prepared? It was not the pitcher's fault because he was doing his job. The curb ball was thrown, but I didn't have to strike at it. Perhaps if I had waited, maybe he may have changed his pitch. But no, I kept striking; so he kept throwing the curb ball. That's exactly the way the devil works. He doesn't have a need to try any new tricks, as long as the old ones are still working. At that moment I received revelation from the Lord. He revealed to me that I was at fault. If I had developed patience and stopped trying to be in such a hurry to do things on my own; perhaps the outcomes would have been different.

All this time I had been thinking life had thrown me a curb ball and it was me all the time. I would become impatient when trying to solve life's problems on my own. I was not not allowing the Lord to help me and that is why I kept striking out. I'm reminded of the scripture in the book of (Isaiah 40:31 KJV) which declares, but they that wait upon the Lord shall renew their strength; they shall mount up with wings as eagles; they shall run and not be weary; and they shall walk, and not faint. If I had been meditating on the word of God, instead of doing things my way; I would have viewed that curve ball entirely differently. I would continue to put myself in certain situations without considering the consequences that would eventually follow. I made some bad choices, but I also knew that the Lord allowed some of these things to happen to gain my attention.

He wanted me to focus on Him. I began to realize that everything is about Him and not about me. As I continue to reflect on my life, my mind goes back to my early childhood. I was born and raised in a small town in Coffee County, Elba, Alabama. My father Billey (Brick) was the only son of

Jeremiah Tank and Naomi Truitt. My mother, Contessa Hurtis Truitt is the second daughter of Tealand and Bonnie Tae Jerkins. The fruit of this union birthed eight children, five girls and three boys. I am the youngest of the five girls.

Growing up in a small town did not provide its residents with much privacy. This was a town where everybody knew, everybody else's business. I don't have the fondest of memories as it pertains to this part of my life. We were poor and lived on the wrong side of the tracks. My daddy drove a pulpwood truck, hauling logs for a man named Roy Ryce. On rainy days my father couldn't work. Any day's he missed because of inclement weather reduced his pay. I remember our family struggling with finances and sometimes we did not have food. My mother worked for Caucasian people as a domestic. What little money she made helped to keep a roof over our heads. The bare necessities were very limited. There were many days that my family had to choose between rent and food.

We resided in Hudson Quarters, in one of many little shotgun houses. Everyone in our community shared the same woes. At times we would have to borrow a cup of sugar or salt from one of our neighbors and they would do the same. Mr. Burling owned a grocery store and would allow us to buy food on credit. When the bill wasn't paid the credit stopped.

I remember when my older brothers would take their home made sling shots, go into the woods behind our house and hunt for wild game. They would come home with rabbits, squirrels, birds and sometimes they would bring home a possum. They would clean them; my sisters would build a fire in the stove with sticks that were gathered from the woods. We would eat and thank God that our bellies were filled for that day. One day our mother came home from work and found rabbit fur, bird feathers and possum hair all over the house. She was very upset with my brothers and forbade them from going into the woods hunting. However, they would still go from time to time if we promised not to tell our mother. They were careful to clean the house much better and got rid of all the evidence before our mother came home. I think she knew that my brothers continued to hunt, but she didn't say anything.

This was our day to day life for a while, until my older brother dropped out of school and started working with our daddy. As I grew older and began to observe my mother's comings and goings, I would notice something. She would come home from work, go into her bedroom and get on her knees to pray. I would hear her crying out to God, asking Him to open doors and make a way for us to have the things we needed to survive. Praying for us to make it through our hardships. Guess what? He answered her prayer and provided for us. We received his grace and continued to buy food from the grocery store. I would see her consistently praying. She would tell us not to worry because the Lord was going to make a way and He did just what she said.

As time moved on we began to see some of the families moving out of Hudson Quarters into better homes and neighborhoods. We would get discouraged because it seemed like we were going to be there forever. Sometimes our mother would sit us down and talk to us about discouragement, disappointment and not having some of the things other people had. She would tell us that being poor didn't define us. She also added that the "things" we did not have, didn't make us less than; and the "things" that others did have didn't make them better than.

My mother stressed to us that our lack of material possessions would help to build our character and make us better people. She taught us that our situations would build us up from the inside out. She told us that despite living in poverty; poverty did not live in us. At the time, I was too young to understand exactly what she was talking about. It was very difficult to stay focused when things didn't seem as if they were getting better. She would continue to tell us that God made us who we were and not to forget it. I thank the

Lord for my mother because she was a powerful, sanctified, Holy Ghost filled; praying woman of God. She not only prayed, but fasted for days and even weeks trusting and believing God's Word.

She instructed us to do the same and would teach us Bible Scriptures to remember. Admonishing us to trust in the Lord and be open for His word to settle in our hearts and not just in our heads. She desired for our lives to be changed for the better. Step by step and day to day; she would motivate us. She fought the spirit of discouragement and did not allow us to hang our heads down. She knew with the help of God that things were going to get better.

As I said before, I was young and didn't understand a lot of what she was saying. However, as I started to mature I began to see that my mother's strong faith was enough to cover me and my family. She never denied the power of God that was working in our lives. As I grew older I began to understand some of the things that she was teaching us. I also personally observed the ways that the Lord was making for us. We truly needed the Lord in order for us to survive during those days.

She continued to keep us in Church and did the best she could in keeping up with our mental and physical development. Sometimes, she would tell us that she couldn't keep up with our minds, but she could keep up with our bodies. I thought she did a pretty good job keeping up with our minds as well. It seemed as if she had eyes behind her head; a woman that was full of wisdom. Sometimes, she could even tell us what we were thinking about doing and say; don't do that. Reminding us that if we delight ourselves in the Lord he would give us the desires of our hearts. I knew those words were in the Bible, but didn't exactly know where they were. I later found them in the book of Psalms. She not only lived the word but prayed and believed the word.

In the book of (Isaiah 55:11 KJV) God said, "So shall my word be that goeth forth out of my mouth: it shall not return unto me void, but it shall accomplish that which I please, and it shall prosper in the thing whereto I sent it." I can truly say, I thank the Lord for a praying and godly mother. I thank the Lord for the strength He gave her to not get tired and give up on me. I'm reminded of the words in the book of (Galatians 6:9 KJV) that reads, " And let us not be weary in well doing: for in due season we shall reap if we faint not." I also thank the Lord for allowing her to live to see her prayers being answered, because she was faithful.

She made sure that we were at church even if no other children were there. We would get upset because some of the other parents weren't as strict with their children as she was with us. She would tell us that she wasn't responsible for their children but only hers. We had to be there every time the church doors were opened. We were there for Bible Band on Tuesday night, Home and Foreign Mission on Thursday night, Pastor's Aid on Friday night, Sunday School on Sunday morning, Sunday Morning Worship Service, Young People Willing Workers on Sunday evening and Sunday Night Worship Service.

Church was the life of my mother as well as for us. We didn't own a vehicle but that did not excuse us from attending services; we walked to church. Our mother would tell us that all excuses were nailed to the Cross when Jesus died and that was the end of that. Through the years I would observe my mother setting the perfect example for her family. She allowed God to work in her life, reminding me that she was the Proverbs 31 virtuous woman. Even though she was strict, she taught us how to love and to look out for one another. I thank the Lord for having a mother like her.

I can remember one Christmas when our grandparents came to our house for a visit. They were living in Jacksonville, Georgia at the time. We were so excited to hear that they were coming because we knew they were bringing us food and other things to eat. That was the first Christmas that I experienced eating my first apple, orange and candy cane. I thought that I had died and went to heaven. That was the best time of my life. I was sad when they had to leave, not because of the things they brought, which I was thankful for, but because they were so much fun. It made me so happy just to be around them. After they left and returned home, our parents gave us the best news I had ever heard in my life. They told us that while our grandparents were there, they went and purchased land. This land was for us to have a house built. We began jumping up and down; thanking and praising the Lord for the blessings that were coming our way.

At that moment I began to think about how our mother was fasting and praying for the Lord to open doors and make a way. She encouraged us to hold on because help was on the way. She didn't know how He was going to do it, but she trusted and believed that He would and He did. Weeks later, our house was being built on the land our grandparents had purchased for us in Mulberry Heights. It was located about a mile from where we were living in Hudson Quarters.

Oh, what a happy day that was when our house was finished and ready for us to move in. I was a young child, but I can vividly remember that special day. We moved what little belongings we had on a wheelbarrow. As we were passing through the neighborhood to get to our new house, the people outside stopped what they were doing and began watching and laughing at us. It didn't matter because we knew that God's hand was upon us and we were moving on up. We finally got settled into our new house and things were getting better for us.

As the years moved on the farmers in the rural counties planted cotton, peanuts, corn and anything else that they could plant. When it was time to harvest the crops they needed workers. The parents that weren't working on other jobs would take their children out to the fields to pick cotton and harvest the crops. Our mother would eventually stop working as a domestic and take me, my older sister and younger brother. The farmers would come to our houses and load up everyone who was willing to go to the fields. The weather didn't stop us from working from sun up to sun down. The fields were hot and we were happy when it started to rain because it meant we didn't have to go back.

Sometimes it took several days before it was dry enough for us to return; at least we had that little break. We would work until all the cotton was picked or pulled, all the peanuts were dug and all the corn was pulled. Nearing the end of harvest season it was soon time to return to school. School started in September, however we didn't return until October. The reason for this is because we needed extra time to buy the things we needed for school. Despite not having all the things we needed and being behind on our schoolwork we somehow made it through and passed to the next grade.

We were still attending church faithfully. Our mother was very strict on us and there weren't many places that we were allowed to go and if it didn't involve church we didn't go. I would hear my older sister say that she would be glad when she was able to get out. Life wasn't all bad; sometimes during the summer our mother would let us visit our grandparents in Jacksonville until it was time to harvest the crops and return back to school.

As time passed a new preacher, Elder T.W. Parris and his wife, Maddie moved to our little town of Elba, Alabama. They later became our pastors. They named the church Parris Temple Church of God in Christ. He came preaching hellfire and brimstone. That salvation comes only by faith in our Lord and Savior Jesus Christ to all that believe on His name and to seek the baptism of the Holy Ghost. He was an anointed powerful man of God. He preached only the word that was in the Bible and his message did not change. Our mother made sure that we were there to hear the word and that we were paying attention to every word that was being preached.

Many people would come to church and hear the word of God being preached and was saved. The church was growing very fast. As the Evangelists were passing through our town the pastor would invite them to preach. Revivals would break out through our region and a mighty move of God took place. People were being saved and filled with the baptism in the Holy Ghost with the evidence of speaking in tongues which was known fully in the Pentecostal movement. I can remember two Evangelists by the name of Elder Benjamin and Elder Samuel coming to our church. Everyone called them the twin preachers. As the Revival continued, people from everywhere were coming. Our church wasn't large enough for all the people. The pastor asked my mother if they could spread a tent in our front yard and have the revival there. She said that she would have to ask my daddy if it was ok and he agreed.

The Revival lasted for weeks. People from all over and all nationalities came together in fellowship to worship and praise the Lord. Once again many people got saved and were filled with the Holy Ghost and with the evidence of speaking in tongues. Many people's lives were changed during those times because they recognized that the presence of the Lord was with us. People that weren't saved began to respect us because they saw things were changing for the better. Many pastors would come and bring their members and fellowship with our church. We could feel the love from all the people because we were all on one accord. As the scripture states,

"And all that believed were together, and had all things common." and as such many were added to the church and were saved.

As time moved on things seemed to be getting a little better. It was time for school to begin. When we were in school I would go to activities such as the movies and parties, but when mama found out about it I would be in trouble. I even wanted to play basketball for our school, but couldn't. When my sister and I would sneak over to the teenage center, a place where young people would gather to dance, listen to music and just have fun; people would see us and tell our parents. Everyone knew we weren't allowed to go there.

Some of the other children would tell us that they were jealous of the way we were being raised. Their parents would allow them to go and do whatever they wanted. We thought what they were saying was crazy. I felt a little better and appreciated the compliment. However, we wanted to be free to go and do the things that they were doing. I sometimes wonder if that was abuse, but couldn't voice my opinion and left it alone; it was part of our Cogic faith.

Maybe they saw some danger in the activities that we couldn't see. My sister would even ask her questions about it and she would quote scriptures. Saying the Bible states, "Wherefore come out from among them, and be ye separate."

We were to live a Godly life. I must honestly say that she was my salvation until I came to know the Lord for myself. I began to read the Bible, study and pray to the Lord for understanding. As I continued to do that, He enlightened me in the scriptures. I understood that the Saints in my day were trying to teach us the ways of the Lord the best way they knew how. I don't think He held it against them for some of the mistakes that were made. Some of those same mistakes are still being made today.

I thank the Lord for my mama instilling values in us and teaching us the importance of standing for what is right. We developed high morals, good attitudes and were better equipped to deal with life on life's terms. Those principles helped bring me to the place where I am today. I made many mistakes along the way, but I can say that it was by the grace and mercy of God that I'm still here. If it had not been for her and the Lord being in my life I don't think I would be here today.

As the years moved on, all of my sisters went their separate ways. My oldest sister dropped out of school and married. She and her husband went to live in Jacksonville, Georgia with our grandparents. My next older sister did the same thing; dropping out of school and also marrying. One exception, she and her husband stayed in Elba, Alabama. My next older sister graduated and was fortunate to attend Alabama State University in Montgomery, Alabama. After completing her studies she moved to Atlanta, Georgia. My older brothers had also married and moved away. One brother moved to Fitzgerald, GA and the other to Bridgeton, NJ. The ones that were left were my next older sister, me and my younger brother.

It was my sister's last year in high school. She was preparing to move to New York and work for a family. One of her teachers spoked to our mother about letting her go. This family was related to the teacher and assured my mom that it would be safe for her to go. Mama said that she would pray about it. As the months passed, graduation came and mama finally told her that she could go. After several days, she received the ticket sent by the family; she left on a Grey Hound Bus. I was sad to see her leave, but glad that she was getting the opportunity to go and have a better life. There weren't any job opportunities here. Many of the young people that graduated went to Detroit, Michigan to work and didn't return.

After a few weeks had passed my mother received a letter from my sister announcing her safe arrival. She stated that she liked it there. The people were very nice and accommodating and she was all settled in. She continued to write to us from time to time. I missed her very much and wished the very best for her. I continued to try and stay focused on finishing school myself.

ॐ The Beginning of the New Life

I finally met a young man that had started attending Mulberry Heights. He was one year my senior and his name was John Davis.

We started talking, showing an interest in each other and I told my mother about him. She said she wanted to meet him and so I asked him to come to my house. After that visit she gave me permission to start dating. It was about time as I was approaching eighteen. Time moved on and we were getting serious about each other. We discussed dropping out of school to get married. I was afraid to mention it to my mother because I knew she wouldn't allow it. I finally got up enough nerves and told her our plans, just like I thought, she said no. She stated that I was going to finish school. I told her that I would go back the following year and finish so she approved.

We began to make plans to get married and we did. On July 3, 1963 we became husband and wife. We were married at my parents' home. My mother made sure that our Pastor Elder T. W. Parris performed the ceremony. The next day was the 4th of July and we moved in with his parents and celebrated our wedding. The next day he had to go to work, despite that fact, I was now beginning the best days of my life because I had just married the love of my life. He later joined my church. He was originally a member of a Baptist church; which didn't believe in the same doctrine. Just because a person goes to church doesn't mean that they are saved. This type of thinking proved to be one of my mistakes.

Three months later I became pregnant with our first child. The plan for going back to school was over. The family was excited about the baby and was helping me to prepare for the arrival. My first baby boy was born the following summer on May 3, 1964. What a joy he was; we named him Courtney and every day was a joy taking care of him. Nine months later I was expecting again. After moving from one place to another, the Lord blessed us with a three bedroom house. The family was growing and we were blessed with a place of our own. We had plenty of room to raise our children in a comfortable environment. Things were going well and on Feb 26, 1965, I had another baby boy. He weighed seven pounds and eleven ounces. We named him Daniel. Those were the happiest days of my life, but things began to change.

I wanted to get a job and help out with the finances, but John didn't think it was a good idea. We had many discussions about it until I mentioned it to my mother and she advised me to wait until my babies were older and started school. That was the end of my thoughts about going to work. I was very busy at home taking care of my two boys, the house and going to church. Things progressed and two years later I was expecting our third child. Another baby boy was born December 2, 1967, we named him Jonathan. He weighed almost eight pounds.

My marriage was changing just as rapidly as my family was growing. John began to change. He was blessed with a better job as a meat cutter at Crimson Packing Company and was making a very good salary. However, he wasn't good at paying the bills. Each week we would get further behind and my parents would help me out when they could. This was causing me to be stressed and it seemed as if John wasn't bothered at all.

I was expecting our fourth child. Baby Jonathan had suddenly taken ill. We rushed him to the hospital where he later died with Spinal Meningitis. The doctor was unsure of the cause. He suspected that the bacteria could have come from John working at the packing company. He was working around hogs and cows and the exposure could have come from there. We were heartbroken and devastated over the loss of our baby boy. It took a while for things to get back to some kind of normalcy. I tried to move on because I had two other sons who needed me. If it had not been for them, my mother,

God and the church family praying, I think that I would have lost my mind. I thank the Lord every day that I didn't.

Later I delivered my fourth child, another son. He weighed eight pounds and three ounces. He helped ease some of the pain that I was living with but couldn't replace baby Jonathan. The memories of him will always be in my heart. Even to this day, I weep for the loss. I'm sure every mother that has lost a child can relate to how I felt. I named my big bundle of joy Hezekiah. I continued to take care of my boys, they brought me so much love and peace. This love and peace filled the void and the pain I was feeling in my heart at that time. I knew the Lord was taking care of me every day, just as I was taking care of them. I thank the Lord for my mother being there keeping us encouraged and letting us know that we could make it. She would tell me that all things work together for the good of them that love the Lord. I didn't understand and couldn't see where the good was in losing my child, but I knew that one day I will understand. By the grace of God I moved on.

As the years passed more changes were taking place. We were hearing rumors about a civil rights movement. The people were marching in protest of the injustice that the Black people were facing. We did not have equal rights and weren't allowed to vote. A preacher by the name of Dr. Martin Luther

King Jr. was leading a large group of people who supported him. These marches were taking place all over the Northern and some Southern cities. The National Association for the Advancement of Colored People (NAACP) as well as other committees and support groups were there to offer their support. There were many young people who also marched to integrate schools and colleges. Many of them were thrown in jail, beaten and murdered for the privilege to have equal rights as well as the opportunity to have a better education and work better jobs.

We wanted a better future. Dr. King led the march to Selma, Alabama. George C. Wallace, the Governor of Alabama stated that he would stand in the door to prevent the Black students from entering the Montgomery, Alabama schools. He was unsuccessful because the students did in fact enter the school.

John F. Kennedy was President during this era and supported this movement by working hard to pass the civil rights bill. Unfortunately, he was assassinated before the bill could be signed. Immediately after President Kennedy's death, Vice President Richard M. Nixon was sworn in as president and shortly thereafter; he signed the civil rights bill. This great movement should have been enough evidence for all people everywhere to know that the Lord does hear and answer prayer. I know that the Saints at my church were praying and I believe that people everywhere were praying for this great movement to be a success. The success of this movement was not without great loss. Dr. Martin Luther King Jr., Alberta King, Medgar Evers, the little girls in the Birmingham, Alabama church bombing and many more whose names are not mentioned.

These people gave their lives so we could have a better one. Which reminds me of the greatest of them all who willingly gave His life. He came down through forty-two generations and walked the earth preaching repentance; for the kingdom of God is at hand. Some people believed and some didn't. Today the same message is being preached. Some believe and some don't, but the message will never change. It is still the same today. As long as the earth shall remain, we should never stop proclaiming the gospel of our Lord and Savior Jesus Christ. We must continue to cry out; repent for the Kingdom of God is at hand. We must never compromise the word of God. There were great sacrifices made for us as a nation of black people to be freed from the hand of the oppressor and the bondage of sin.

It is very sad to say, but there are many of us that still choose to stay in bondage and live a life of sin rather than rising up and moving forward. Grabbing hold of the great opportunity that has been provided for us. Today, I can say that it's never too late and we are never too old to rise up and make things happen for ourselves. If some of you have been complaining or trying to make excuses for why things haven't worked out for you, stop and think about it for a minute. Maybe you were trying to do it on your own or waiting for someone to do it for you. Maybe you didn't do some of the things that I mentioned, or for some other reason, maybe you didn't acknowledge God in it and did it your way.

After the great civil rights movement things began to get better for everyone. The people were able to vote, the schools and colleges were being integrated and the white only signs came down. The people were getting better jobs and qualifying for programs that were offered to minority families. These changes provided a better life with more security and less stress.

Yes, things got better for my family as well. My daddy was employed as a driver for a Sanitation Department and my mother was employed at a hospital working in the Dietary Department. Many of the townsmen were employed working at Patsy Trailers Inc. and later they also began to employ women. Companies begin to bring their businesses to town. Factories were built to employ workers. Later a textile sewing factory was also built and started employing workers.

With all of the new opportunities I was excited about my future. I waited until my boys started school just like my mother advised. Then I applied for a job at a local factory and began working. By this time John felt a little better about me going to work. As the months went by I discovered that I was expecting again and worked almost up to the time of my delivery. I gave birth to an eight pound, three ounce baby girl. I named her Jahzara which means (African Princes) and that's what she was to me.

The whole community was shocked because they were accustomed to me giving birth to boys. My response was, to God be the glory; for the things He has done. She was a joy to everyone in the family and especially to my mama. She wanted our baby girl to stay with her all the time. By this time mama had retired from the hospital and was home babysitting for other women in the community as they started to work. Not only did my mother love spending time with her, my sisters did too. As she grew older we discovered that the Lord had blessed her with a beautiful singing voice. Both our family and church family would have her singing for them all of the time.

As the years rolled by, my marriage continued to decline. I didn't know what to do. At times I would hear rumors that John had a girlfriend. I kept my head in the sand and continued to take care of our children and our home. I kept working at the factory and going to church. I would receive advice from my mother and church family from time to time. I continued to trust God the best that I could. I realized that life can sometimes become overwhelming and that it causes us to lose our focus. When our focus shifts, we can stop depending on and trusting in God. Even when I tried to refocus and trust God, things only seemed to get worse.

John began to get abusive, more controlling, demanding and he stopped going to church. At times he would tell me that I couldn't attend services. I thought to myself, Lord, what am I going to do? I would run to my mother again for advice. She would tell me to just go to the morning services and stay home for the evening and night services. I did as she said, but it didn't make me feel any better because I thought that it was wrong for him to stop me from going to church. I obeyed him, but deep down in my heart I felt that some of the things he was doing weren't right. His actions and treatment towards me was unjust, but I was afraid to take a stand against what he was doing. I just kept quiet and continued to put up with it.

I tried to feel better and condone the way I was being treated. At the very least the children and I were still able to attend church services and participate in the activities. That was the only life we had besides going to my mother's house.

We enjoyed being with her and our family. Sometimes my mind would reflect back to when John and I first got married. I wondered if it was love or lust. Even though I thought I was living right in the eyes of God, maybe I got married for the wrong reason. Maybe I just wanted to get out from under my mother's strong discipline and do things on my own, like my other sisters.

Sometimes I would be so confused and burdened down until I just didn't know what to do. The only thing that kept me from losing my mind was a praying mother, my precious children and the Lord looking after me. As I look back I can understand why God blessed me with such a precious daughter with a beautiful voice. When she was old enough to start school, she would sometimes participate in the school chorus. She was even selected to sing solos. At church she would also sing in the Junior Choir and was the selected soloist for church programs. My daughter blessed the entire community with her heavenly voice. As a matter of fact, God blessed all of my children with singing voices.

My sons would participate in the church activities and sing as well. They formed their own group and named it *"Able"*. It is Elba (Alabama) spelled backwards. Their group would participate in community activities and perform for both local and neighboring churches. They also traveled to

Jacksonville, Florida to participate in singing competitions where they won several awards.

Both John and I were blessed with singing voices. However, he did not make his talent a public thing. Singing became a part of our family and we enjoyed it. Sometimes when I would feel down, I think Zara, which was Jahzara's nickname, could sense how I was feeling. She would start singing with that anointed voice. She would sing some of Vickie Winans' songs and lift my spirit. Her voice ushered in the presence of the Lord and it blessed my soul. The way I was feeling disappeared. I thank God every day for blessing me with such precious children.

As the months passed I became pregnant with my sixth child. I gave birth to a seven pound, seven ounce, bouncing baby boy. We named him Tevin. He was the last one because the doctor informed me that if I kept having babies it could potentially cause health problems. He discussed a procedure that could potentially prevent me from having more children. I discussed it with John and other family members and we all agreed that it would be best for me. With all of us on the same page, I decided to go ahead and have the procedure done.

The procedure that I am referring to is tubal ligation. I wanted to stay healthy and take care of my children. Not much changed. When things would get too hard I would bundle up the kids, go to my parents and stay with them for a while. My daddy didn't have very much to say about me leaving John because he had also heard rumors about infidelity. While staying with my parents John would worry me until we returned home.

This was the last time that I would run to my mother during times of marital difficulties. While staying there, I had come to the realization that she had set a standard for what marriage was. Growing up, I noticed that my mama didn't talk very much about what was going on in her marriage. Not that she was in denial, she would just pray and leave it in the hands of the Lord. I started doing the same; I prayed and stopped running to mama about it. Not that it would do any good anyway; I already knew what she was going to say. Realizing that mama had brought me as far as she could and it was time for me to start standing on my own. I had to begin to fully trust in the Lord.

I must admit, there were still times when I tried to handle our problems on my own because I thought the Lord wasn't working fast enough but I only made a mess of things. Sometimes the boys would come home from school and tell me the gossip that they heard about their daddy and his girlfriend. I confronted him, he would deny it and wanted to know who told me. I didn't want to get the boys into any trouble so I just left it alone and continued to stay with him. I would hear the older people say an old piece of a man was better than not having one at all. I thought within myself that they didn't know what they were talking about.

My mother would quote scriptures to me about how the wife was to stay at home, love her children, take care of her husband, love and obey him. I knew that she was trying to keep me encouraged and teach me the best that she knew because that was the doctrine of our church. If I stayed, I had to abide by it. Trying to be obedient and believe that I was doing the right thing; that's what I did. I began praying and seeking God for a way out if it was His will. During those times, something very unusual happened.

A flood came through our little town and water was everywhere. People's homes, schools and businesses were flooded. Everyone was devastated by the destruction that it left behind. It took several years for things to get back to normal, but Elba was never the same.

Several years passed and my mother became very ill and suffered a massive stroke and later passed away at the Elba General Hospital. I can't express the heartbreak, pain and the loss that I experienced during the days that followed. It seemed like a dream and I was hoping that I would wake up, but it didn't happen. I felt as if part of me was gone. I was empty, void and walked around in a daze. I couldn't even think straight. I know I said this before, but it bears repeating. I truly do thank the Lord for my children. They were there for me, along with other people in the community. Everyone knew how close our family was. My mama had made a big impact in the community over the years.

We finally made it through the funeral. I was trying to get back to normal, but my mama death caused me to think seriously about the days ahead. I tried to continue doing things as usual but everything had changed. My children went their separate ways. My oldest son had finished high school and moved to Montgomery, Alabama. The next oldest moved to Enterprise, AL.

I continued to work at the factory and one year later one of my sisters passed away. She had been dealing with a number of health problems. One problem in particular was related to complications from a kidney transplant. She passed away at the U.A.B. Hospital in Birmingham, Alabama. More heartbreak and loss, but through it all the Lord gave us strength to make it through those stressful times and life went on.

As time moved on the Lord blessed us with another house. This one was a four bedroom home in the suburbs; which we called the country. I must say that the Lord was still blessing us even in the midst of what was going on in our marriage. We sold the house in town and moved into our new home. Everything seemed to be going alright, but John still wasn't bringing home enough money to take care of all the bills.

Jahzara was in her last year of school and working part time. When she finished school she was fortunate to attend Montgomery of Alabama State University. She later moved to New York City to live with one of her aunts. Eventually, she returned home and began working. She started participating in church activities and eventually became the Director of the Choir until she met the love of her life Calvin Jones. They attended school together but had no idea that one day they would be in a relationship.

Everyone was surprised when they heard about their marriage, even his mother. She knew that they were dating and that they had plans to get married. Both of our families were attending the same church and knew one another very well, but I guess she just brushed it off and didn't think anything else about it.

One day Calvin went and joined the army and after basic training he came back and they were married. Everyone was surprised when they announced it one Sunday morning during the church services. Zara continued to live in Elba because she was now pregnant with her first baby and wanted to stay close to the family while waiting to give birth. I took her to the hospital where she delivered a very alert baby boy. His eyes were wide open as he looked around at the world. The doctors and nurses were surprised.

They said that they had never seen anything like that before. After a few days in the hospital I brought them home and they stayed with me for a few months. Calvin returned from Camp Shelby, Mississippi and was later stationed at Ft. Stewart, GA. After Zara and the baby joined Calvin, it was very lonely around the house. I didn't know what to do with myself, especially after Tevin, our youngest and last son graduated and joined the Alabama National Guard. I was now an empty nester, but I still had my job at the factory.

I continued attending church which kept me from being too lonely. One day I received a letter in the mail which stated that our house was going into foreclosure because of non-payment. I was devastated because I foolishly trusted that John was paying the mortgage. At this point I was tired of struggling with him and all the things that he was taking me through. I called my daughter and discussed with her what happened. She told me to pray to the Lord and wait for an answer before making a decision. After a few days the answer came.

◈ The Strength to Move Beyond What I Can See

One Sunday a preacher and his wife were passing through town going home to New Orleans, Louisiana and visited our church. He was the pastor of the church where my daughter and son-in-law were the minister of music and choir director. Our Pastor invited him to preach during the Sunday Night Service. His subject was *"prepare for the journey"* and his scripture came from the book of (Genesis 12:1 KJV), where the Lord spoke to Abram and said, "Get thee out of thy country, and from thy kindred, and from thy father's house, unto a land that I will shew thee." Despite not knowing where he was going, Abram obeyed the Lord. Doing the service that night I received my answer from the Lord and knew exactly what I was going to do.

The next day I called my daughter and told her what happened and that I had finally made my decision to leave John and relocate. She asked me where I was going and I told her that I didn't know but I had to leave. After a few days I started packing up my things and began to prepare for my journey. John asked me what I was doing and I told him that I was leaving and this time I wouldn't be coming back. He tried quoting scriptures to me about how the wife was supposed to stay with her husband. I didn't even try to argue with him concerning the scriptures. Because we both knew that he only used the word of God to manipulate me. Despite knowing what he was supposed to do, he failed to take care of his family.

Several days passed and my daughter called me. She told me that she and Calvin had discussed my situation and asked me if I would consider moving to Ft Stewart, GA. I thought about it and after a while I accepted their offer. I eventually discussed the situation with my pastor and shared with him the decision that I made. He said that he understood and was sorry that I was leaving. Knowing the magnitude of the situation, he gave me his Blessing.

On January 8, 1995 I quit my job at the factory. Several days later my son-in-law and daughter came, loaded all of my things in the moving truck and we left. John was able to convince our daughter and son-in-law that he was going to do better if they allowed him to join us. I didn't believe him. I learned over the years that locations don't change anybody. The change must come from within. I knew that he wasn't ready to change, but I didn't argue and went along with their decision.

We arrived at Ft. Stewart and settled into our new place, started attending church and John was hired at Kroger's grocery store as a meat cutter. Things were going well. We found a house in Hinesville close to where he was working. We once again moved into our new home. I got a job working in the school system. After a while things went right back to the way they always were. John once again became slack with paying the bills. The utilities were disconnected and the rent wasn't paid. I discovered that he had found another girlfriend. Like all the others before her, she was now the one who was getting his money.

I thought that it was about time for me to learn some sense. After all these years I continued to go along with the program. Things failed to get better and I was getting nowhere. It was finally time for me to take a stand and look out for myself. I knew the children were trying to help him to do better, but that didn't work. He has always wanted to do; what he wants to do. It was time for me to look out for myself.

For so long I was trying to please people and do what I thought was right. This time I had finally made up my mind that this was it. I went out looking for a place of my own. As I waited for the people to get back in touch with me, I was constantly praying for the Lord to make a way. Because I had made so many mistakes in the past I was hoping that I was making the right decision. As I sat thinking about what I was planning to do, I was reminded of the scripture that I had read in the book of (Galatians 5:1 KJV) which declares, "Stand fast therefore in the liberty wherewith Christ hath made us free, and be not entangled again with the yoke of bondage." The Holy Ghost ministered to me that day about how people will try to keep me in bondage, but Jesus came to set me free.

I'm also reminded of another scripture that Jesus spoke in the book of (John 8:32 KJV) and this is what He said, "And ye shall know the truth, and the truth shall make you free." Finally, that was enough for me. I understood that I could pray all day, read my Bible and believe Him for the answer, but until I get up and make things happen for myself it will never come to pass.

Another scripture also said in the book of (James 2:17 KJV), "Even faith, if it hath no works, is dead, being alone." I remembered something someone said, that there are three types of people, those that wait for things to happen, those that watch things happen and those that make things happen. Today I'm one of those people that make things happen.

Praise the Lord, He blessed me with my own house. I moved out of the house with John, left him sitting right there and I continued to work in different schools. Several weeks later I received a telephone call and it was John, asking me if he could come and stay with me for a few days until he could get his own place. I was very shocked to hear those words, but I guess I shouldn't have been. Of all the years that we were married, he never took his responsibilities as a man seriously.

I told him no and that is when trouble started. He would harass me over the phone and I eventually had to get the number changed. He would come to my place of work and try to talk to me, but I ignored him. This went on for days until one of my sons came to stay with me. They feared that he would try and harm me in some sort of way. They were right.

He found out where I was living, came over one night and kicked the door down. When I reached for the phone to call the police, he told me what he would do if I continued to make the call. His words struck fear in my heart. Tevin was in his room and came out when he heard all the commotion. As he reached for the phone to call the police, John attacked him; stabbing him in the arm and chest. Then he ran out of the house. Tevin was bleeding everywhere. I ran to the phone and called the police and told them what had happened.

They arrived with the paramedics, bandaged him up and rushed us to the hospital. The police followed us there and I gave them a report of what happened. A short time later they reported that they had found John. He was arrested and charged for attempted murder. Tevin was stabilized. We were told by the doctors that we were very Blessed because one of the injuries was close to a main artery. Had we waited several more minutes he could have bled to death. I don't think that I would have forgiven myself.

I thanked the Lord for keeping him alive. He stayed in the hospital for several days. He shared with me that his daddy had called and asked for forgiveness and he forgave him. The police let John out of jail until his trial, but he was forbidden to come anywhere near us. Tevin told the police that he didn't want to press charges against his father. However the police informed us that the State was going to pick up the charges. John was going to have to go to trial for what he had done to his son. I brought Tevin home from the hospital and I prayed everyday for his healing. He eventually recovered from the wounds. I would check on him at night and noticed a butcher knife under his pillow and a baseball bat by his bed. I knew that he was afraid that his daddy may try to come back and do both of us harm. My daughter tried to get us to go to counseling, but decided against it.

Maybe we should have considered talking to someone about the situation. Finally John's trial day came and the lawyer told us we didn't have to be there if we didn't want to. We decided as a family not to go. When the trial was over, John was sentenced to five years probation and he also had to pay Tevin restitution.

I continued to pray that the Lord would remove the fear from my son's heart. I couldn't help but think that there were other things that may also be going on inside of him; causing him pain. I blame myself for the physical pain he suffered. I hope and pray that he would not hold it against me.

My children would tell me to leave, but I stayed hoping that one day things would get better, but instead they got worse. I thank the Lord that it didn't take death for me to realize that the marriage was over. I find myself weeping when I think about what could have happened. I continuously thank the Lord because it was only by His Grace, Mercy and Love that we are still here. It's only Him that kept us and is keeping us alive.

After that ordeal with John, we were divorced and didn't see each other anymore. I heard through the children that he had married one of the women that he was dating when we were married. I finally have peace within myself and no regrets. I am still thanking and praising the Lord for the new life that He has given me.

My everyday prayer is, "Lord when it seems like I can't hold on to you please hold on to me." I believe that He will because His word tells me that He will never leave me nor forsake me. I'm depending on that and I will always be grateful for the people that surrounded me and helped me get back on my feet. I was given another house to live in already furnished and Tevin met a wonderful girl that was there for him. They later married and moved to Virginia.

I'm trying to put the past behind me and move forward. I sometimes still allow fear to set me back; still afraid that I will make the wrong choices. I have to quickly remove those thoughts from my mind and continually trust God. Constantly remind myself of the new life that I'm living. It's not about me, but all about Him.

I joined the church where my daughter and her family were a part of the ministry of music. I began working in the ministry and later the Pastor appointed me one of the adult Sunday School teachers. After several years passed I became an Ordained Minister of the Gospel. Preaching and teaching the word of God.

I enjoyed working in both the ministry and the schools. I had settled into my new life until I suffered an injury at work. I was cleaning class rooms and suddenly I bent over and couldn't stand back up. The supervisor took me to the hospital, tests were taken and it was revealed that I had osteoporosis. This diagnosis caused me to quit my job and go on disability. I moved out of my house, into an apartment which was more convenient for me. I began taking medicine for my bone condition and continued to move on.

At the time of writing this book Thanksgiving was right around the corner. I will be preparing a special dinner for my family and some of my friends. I am looking forward to seeing my children and grandchildren once again. I'm also looking forward to enjoying them in the future. Many years have passed, I have lost many loved ones, including my ex-husband John. Praise be to God I have one remaining brother.

Evangelist Shirley Pruitt

ॐ Words of Encouragement

By the grace of God, He has Blessed me to move forward. I am still attending church, working in ministry and teaching His Word. I truly enjoy the presence of the Lord; meditating on His Word and being mindful of Psalm 37:4 that declares, "Delight yourself in the LORD, And He shall give you the desires of your heart." If I do that, whatever I ask of Him; "I will not be denied."

My advice is to forget about all the excuses, failures and mistakes you've made in the past. Concentrate on the now. Allow me to encourage you at this moment by saying, I was just where you are. I thought that all was lost. I had done all of this and all of that and didn't see any evidence of my hard work. I had put my all into my family and with the exception of being blessed with my five lovely children; I was dismayed with life. Like I've said at the beginning of this book, I was tired, drained and had no energy left. I had given until I was depleted and I thought all was lost.

I can now testify with all assurity that it's not over until God says it's over. It's time for us to stop thinking about what could have happened, or what should have happened; but didn't. Yesterday is gone, just like the psalmist said and tomorrow may never be mine. I've decided to take it one day at a time. I hope and pray that you will do the same and allow the Lord to do the rest. Allow Him to speak to you. Be obedient to His Word, do just what He says and you won't go wrong. I would like to repeat the words that God spoke to Jeremiah while the children of Israel were in captivity in Babylon. God had caused them to tarry there because of their disobedience. This is what the Lord said in Jeremiah 29:11 (NKJV), "For I know the thoughts that I think toward you, says the LORD, thoughts of peace and not of evil, to give you a future and a hope."

We sometimes place ourselves in situations that cause us to feel defeated. These situations can also hinder our blessings. We might even want to blame others, but we need to remember God gave us all free will. This provision allows us the freedom to choose. We need to be mindful that there are consequences that follow every choice or decision that we make.

I sit and think about some of the bad choices that I have made down through the years. I know that with the help of the Lord I will not be doing them again and I'm sure you won't either. There is one thing that we do know, we can't change the things that have been, but we sure can change the way we think now. I think about it often, that if I had paid attention and allowed the Word of God to direct me in some of the decisions I made, perhaps I may have had better outcomes. Instead, I did it my way and that is the inspiration for writing this book.

I thought about the direction in which my life was headed. I made up my mind that I would not be denied. I will not deny God from fulfilling the plans that He has for my life. Allowing His Word to transform me and renew my mind daily. This reminds me of the words the Apostle Paul told the new converts at Rome. Romans 12:1-2 (NKJV) which declares, "I beseech you therefore, brethren, by the mercies of God, that you present your bodies a living sacrifice, holy, acceptable to God, which is your reasonable service. And do not be conformed to this world but be transformed by the renewing of your mind, that you may prove what is that good and acceptable and perfect will of God."

Let us be mindful to first acknowledge God when making choices or decisions. Whatever you are planning to do, think it through carefully, don't be in a hurry and pay attention to that quiet voice. He will tell you everything you need to know, say or do. He will direct your path (Proverbs 3:6). I thank God every day for giving me another chance and this time I'm going to do it His way. If you can relate to what I'm saying I hope and pray that you will do the same. Scripture declares in the book of Isaiah 40:31 (KJV), " But they that wait upon the Lord shall renew their strength; they shall mount up with wings as eagles; they shall run, and not be weary; and they shall walk, and not faint."

Remember that there is a process you must go through because you do not want to continue to make those same mistakes over and over again. Take your time and allow the Lord to make the changes that need to be made in you. One day you will be glad you did and remember that life still goes on.

I have to remind myself of these Scriptures daily. Many things will come, causing me to lose focus on what the Lord has promised me. I would sometimes doubt if these things would come to pass but I had to let go of the doubt and get my focus back. I'm sure you have experienced the same thing, but don't give up; just look up. Ask the Lord to give you the strength to make it through the day. I'm also reminded of Psalm 46:1 (NKJV) which declares, "God is our refuge and strength, A very present help in trouble." Therefore we will not fear. I encourage you to apply the Scriptures that I have presented in this book. Apply them to your everyday living and you will be amazed at the transforming power of God that will take place in your life.

As you prepare yourself for your journey, let the Lord take the lead and allow His Word to become a lamp unto your feet and a light unto your path (Psalm 119:105). Follow along and get to know Him. You will begin to understand that whatsoever you ask of Him according to His will, it will not be denied.

To be continued...

Evangelist Shirley Pruitt

www.ingramcontent.com/pod-product-compliance
Lightning Source LLC
Chambersburg PA
CBHW051333150726
47997CB00004B/1455